THE FOUR ELEMENTS

WE ARE EARTH MOTHER

By

Marcus Nobreus

Cover design by: Skyler Kenny

Library of Congress Control Number:

Printed in the United States of America

Title Page

For the Love of Pachamama,
Ombute Devi and my mother, Birgitta Allroth.

FOREWORD

At about 10,000 feet in the Eastern Sierras, a mountain range in California, I sat down and I posed this question to the Rock People and Pachamama: "How are we all connected?"

Ancient teachings claim that even a rock has consciousness, that everything in existence carries this consciousness of which we are part. I was curious how that made sense.

The answers came to me in that meditation and in many more after that. I learned to listen, to truly listen to the wordless messages that come in form of images or intuitive knowings, and I began to see the world in a completely new light.

Do yourself a favor and sit with a tree. As you do, move your attention to the tree, feel into how the tree actually experiences our world. What does the world look like when you don't have eyes the way humans do, is it made up of colors and vibrations or maybe tones? How does a tree experience the world?

And then, as you sit by a lake, become the lake, feel, sense, experience the world as the lake.

This way we can expand our view of the world and we understand more of our fellow beings and their experience of life. I will discuss how we are all made up of the elements of our home, Earth Mother. How we already consists of and are made up by; air, water, earth and fire.

First I will point out how you and I are made up of these particles and molecules and then how you can practically assimilate behaviors and traits to increase your awareness with the elements. And finally, meditations upon each element.

Introduction

How is this book going add to your life? Why would just you go through the trouble of reading it?

This book is meant to show you how you are connected to Earth Mother herself and how we are but one part of a huge energy system that makes up the organism of our planet.

I walk you into the world of connection, showing you how we actually are physically, energetically and spiritually connected to Pachamama (Earth Mother).

I do this so we all can learn what it means to be human and to bring to the forefront of our awareness that we are just one piece in the huge, complex puzzle of Life that makes up Earth Mother. My intention is that this will help to remove feelings of separation, division and guide you towards your spiritual awakening and deepen your walk.

Humanity. The species that invaded its own host, the species that forgot the connection to its own mother, Earth Mother or Pachamama.

For 200,000 years (or so) we lived as one with nature. We had certain dwellings called cities, but they were nothing like our modern cityscapes or city living. Nowadays we believe we are civilized because we live in houses that look like boxes; we drive vehicles that pollute and isolate us and we live in ways where our greatest dream is to please others.

What we call civilization, my spiritual teacher and shaman Ombute calls domestication; I call it savagery.

Looking back on history, at what the Europeans called savages, we see that the real savagery was committed by the conquistadores: the Spanish, English, French and other European colonialists who invaded and subdued millions of other peoples. These settlers went into the Americas, African continent and the East. The European idea of enlightenment and domestication was ground for the incredible injustices in the North American tradition of slavery, in the bloody conquest of North and South America, and on the great nation of India and the whole continent of Africa.

As we examine our behavior from a more somber point of view, it is plain to see that humans have acted inhumanely towards each other and other sentient beings for thousands of years.

Why is that?

What drives our thinking to be so inclined that we believe to have the right to enslave other humans and other species?

The short answer is disconnect. We are disconnected from our origin, from Earth Mother and from a compassionate, natural, connected way of life and in which we have created a need for more. More of everything.

The need for more - more things, more money, more security, more safety, more love, more sex, has not always been a part of the human psyche. If you break down that need for more you find fear. The fear of not having enough, not belonging, not feeling loved, is the driving force behind so many of our either conscious or unconscious, destructive behaviors. This fear of not having enough is based in the disconnect humans have become accustomed to and call civilization.

For many thousand of years we were able to keep a healthy balance, both within our own tribes and with our surrounding nature. When humans spend more time with Earth Mother, in nature, we learn the deeper lessons contained in every tree, blade of grass and from the clouds and the ocean.

Look at yourself and your experience, go out and sit in a park or better yet, in the wild, and experience how different you feel at the end of the day. You have learned many new insights, feel refreshed and renewed and you have grown in your understanding of your part to play.

But instead we spend less and less time in nature. Many of us grow up in concrete jungles across our globe. In the cities the rules for survival are different and they are based in mind.

The world we have created is almost only based in the "haves" and the "have nots". This is of course a fear based way of looking at our world and not how Earth provides for us if we let Her.

If we let her provide us with food and water without interference from our money driven thought process we could still be eating healthy, non-processed, non-toxic foods and water.

What is the difference today?

The main difference is that we see ourselves as masters of our planet; we believe ourselves to be so intelligent and successful that we can take whatever piece of land we want and keep it as "ours". If you break down the concept of owning land, you soon realize how ridiculous the concept is. Who did you pay to own this piece of land? The previous owner? And to whom did he or she pay? Who paid the Earth itself, Earth Mother, for the land? How can a country or a person claim a piece of land for itself? Did they pay rent or a bill of sale to Earth Mother? Do we pay dividends to the Sun for the power and life source that it provides for us? Or the rivers, or the ocean for all the food?

If an ant said "this land here, with this ant hill on it, is mine, and you humans cannot walk here", would we listen? Would we respect if a deer, bear or wolf came to us and said: "I have paid for this piece of land in berries or in other forms of natural currencies, so this land is now mine and you have no right to be here?" Would we respect that? Of course not. Our hubris knows no limits.

Are we so egocentric and ethnocentric that it is only when humans lay claim to a piece of land that we count it as true, as having merit?

We have taken the seat of dominance on Earth without truly realizing what it means. We don't understand that being a "crown of creation" or "king/queen" means to be a custodian and caretaker of our home, not an abuser and killer.

In what currency do we pay Earth Mother, our own mother for the gift of life? We have to face our role in this drama of life. We have to face that fear - the insecurity and hunger for power and safety - has put us on an egomaniacal, destructive and psychopathic path. We have to acknowledge this and redirect our ways —compassionately, intelligently and truthfully - to a type of living that is in tune with and in harmony with the very nature of Earth Mother.

The purpose of this book is to point out how You and I already are Nature, we are Earth Mother herself.

I Am Water

1. You Are Water

E very part of your body is affected by water. You drink, absorb, and live in water. Even the air contains 2-3% water.

From the moment you are formed in the womb you are encapsulated in amniotic fluid, a form of water containing life essential properties. You depend on water for your survival until the moment you die. You also depend on water for all parts of your survival, as in drinking, cleaning, washing, and comfort.

Many large cities sprung up around water, be it oceans or rivers. All the ancient cities were accessible by water, as this was the main way of transporting goods and people.

Physically speaking

You are Water. Your body is made up of the H2O molecule to a large degree. Your brain contains about 76% and the lungs about 83% and your whole physical being; blood flow, energetic pathways, lymphs and joints, need water to function properly.

Much like the rainforest or any other part of Earth Mother: too little water, you get desert, too much water results in swamp lands, transitioning either to land or to water. The systems of Earth Mother work in balance with each other and they are self-regulating.

The biosphere you live in is much like a lake or any enclosed system. When the balance is thrown off you get dysfunction in the system. The acidity/alkalinity balance gets thrown off, resulting in that plant and animal life dies off.

This goes for your body as well. You need to maintain a healthy level of water in your system. This is where certain things you ingest aid in keeping the water balance and others don't.

The, oh so popular, coffee drink is one of those. Coffee itself is not harmful, but the way many people drink it and the way many of us use it to get energy, becomes very harmful for our physical body. Let's call it "caffeining" (sic.). It feeds the energetic pathways in your system and helps you to focus and to stay on task, but to a price. An overproduction of cortisol in your adrenal glands causes adrenal fatigue over time.

This makes your body use the hollow energy of the "fight-or-flight" system, as well as blocking adenosine, which causes sleepiness.

Adrenaline is helpful in short spurts, in emergency situations, but in our modern day society, we live with the kicks of high adrenaline every day; leading to difficulty sleeping, focusing and often feeling very tired. The high levels of adrenaline wears you down over time and create an overstressed system, resulting in a fatigued, acidic body. This is not only caused by caffeine, but it is part of the price of an over-productive and over-pressurized existence.

When you learn to either stop or regulate your caffeine you become healthier on many physical, emotional and energetic levels and it is easier to find peace within yourself.

We live in a dehydrated and overstressed state which is the main cause of many modern day diseases. Our overall life style is the perpetrator combined with the toxins in our food, water and air.

According to the Japanese author Masaru Emoto*[1], you also influence the properties of the molecules of the water in your body with your intention and emotional state.

In short, if you are angry or negative, full of spite or anxiety, your mindset affects and changes the structure of the water molecules in your body, thereby making the water in your body less efficient in its life-giving and cleansing properties.

Masaru Emoto studied the effect of prayer and love versus the effect of anger and hate shown towards water in petri dishes and found a huge difference between the different water batches. After exposing the water dishes to either love and prayer or hate and anger he froze the water and then studied it under a microscope. His findings are available in the book "The Hidden Messages in Water".

The differences in the images of water that was exposed to hate and negativity and the ones exposed to love and positivity are remarkable. They show the value of self-love and appreciation as a means to keep your body healthy.

The different results also show the connection between your psyche and your physical body. How does your self-talk sound? Do you curse yourself out when you are late for an appointment, or if you stub your toe or forget something?

Since our bodies are primarily made up of water molecules our self-talk severely affects our health and immune system.

Is this scientifically proven in peer-reviewed studies? No.

Do I believe these studies to be valid in spite of this? Yes.

I know you have an impact on your energy field with your intention. I also know that you can change the molecular structure of your cells with your emotional state and with your intent. You can easily try this for yourself.

Think of something that makes you really angry, right now. Feel what happens in your body. Or recall one of the times when you have really lost it. Or the sad times of losing a loved one.

When you recall that feeling it is quite easy to realize that this affects our physical being as well. Just like when we are under threat, when we are being attacked our whole body fills up with different stress hormones to help us access more power, strength and sharp thinking to help us survive.

Or better yet, recall the beautiful feeling of being deeply in love.

Observe what happens in your body, how it feels. When you pay attention to how these different states feel, you connect the dots between your different emotional states and your wellbeing, both physical, emotional, mental and spiritual.

When you look at yourself in an honest light you will see that a certain feeling dominates your life more than others.

You are often either sad, happy, angry, negative, positive, or a balance between all of them.

This affects every area of your life, both your outside world, your emotional state, and your physical and mental being. And this state definitely affects how you carry yourself physically. It is easy to see that you carry your emotional state in your face and in your posture.

According to the American biologist Bruce Lipton, PhD, *[2] even your DNA and the protein in the cell nucleus are impacted by your emotional states and stress levels.

I believe you shape the reality you experience, even your physical reality. This is why modern spiritual traditions speak of us as co-creators when we are aligned with our higher vibration. When you speak negatively about yourself, (yes, cussing yourself out counts as negative self talk...), your negative intention creates an energetic response in your body, causing damage to the water molecules in our bodies, creating more negative feelings. This, in turn, impacts your immune system in a negative way. Your cells grow weaker as a result and this allows disease to grab hold in your system.

A negative state of mind fuels more of the same feeling, as well as you see what you look for, with the result that you feel more and more powerless, since you have less power available in your system.

My personal experience found me, at age 22, going through a deep grieving process as I was disconnecting from my dysfunctional upbringing, I went to the ocean every day for two months and dipped my head and body under water. This process of cleansing in the ocean became an extremely healing experience and I learned the value of self-baptizing and releasing trauma with the help of the healing and grounding effects of the ocean.

The negative ions in the ocean help relieve depression and other heavy energies in our system. They also aid our body in producing serotonin and remove both oxidants and positive ions. An abundance of positive ions causes inflammation, acidity and disease.

The embrace of water has many healing aspects for humans. You feel held and comforted in water and you cleanse your energy body when you take a shower or a bath. Over-sensitive individuals, hyper-sensitive people (HSP), and people with certain types of diagnosis, do well from submerging themselves under water. The dulling of the senses helps an oversensitive person or a person with ADHD to feel safe and contained.

When an overstimulation of the senses is the problem, the submerging of oneself in water helps to slow the input of information. But you don't need a diagnosis to feel safe in water. This is why so many love taking baths, submerged in the life-giving fluid.

Spiritually speaking

According to science, life originated in the oceans. The ocean carries your original energetic imprint and has a way of returning you to health when you immerse yourself in it.

Dipping yourself in water functions as a reset of your system. When you allow the healing powers of Mother Ocean clear away your sorrows and the debris from your past, you move energies that previously have been stuck.

This is where the idea of baptism, practiced in several religions and spiritual movements, fills a great function and connects you back with original Spirit.

Water is fluid, all encompassing and life-giving.

When you learn to accept "what is" and the persistent pervasive nature of water, which can erode even the biggest rock over time, you recognize the energetic power of water.

Water is Life and at the same time, water just "is". Water teaches you acceptance and perseverance.

The fluidity of water shows you how energy moves through our world. When you throw a pebble in a lake and the rings spread out in all directions so does a kind or helpful act.

If you were able to see how far a wave of emotion travels within our human community you would learn just how big of an effect you have on our whole collective field of consciousness.

As an example, imagine that you hold the door for someone at the airport. They smile and say thank you and you feel better about your day. Then perhaps the person you held the door for also feels a bit more encouraged about human kind. They get into a cab and instead of completely disregarding the driver they may strike up a conversation. And they may tip better because they are in a good mood. So the driver feels better about him- or herself and because of this they are happier with the rest of their clients, which results in a better day for everyone. And when the driver comes home, he or she may be kinder to their children.

This chain of event can potentially take place due to the kind act you showed a complete stranger at the airport.

Konrad Lorenz, an Austrian zoologist, *[3] studied the behaviors of animals. When he studied jackdaws and how they behaved he learned that the whole clattering (group) reacted to a mutual feeling in the whole clattering, not to a specific leader.

Previously it was believed that jackdaws had a leading bird, a chief, that called out decisions.

Lorenz's studies showed that when any one of the jackdaws felt a certain feeling and made the sound of that feeling, that emotion spread through out the whole clattering and they all took off in unison. So when one felt fear, it made the fear sound and the others felt the same feeling.

Compare this to human laughter. When you hear a human laugh it is often irresistible to not join in. Or when you hear crying or yelling. You feel the feelings of the expression and then fall into that frequency.

Look at the movements in our world today, look at how many people feel and tap into anger and then join forces with others who feel the same. This is how energy spreads.

And when you stay spiritually centered you set the tone inside of you and you then can choose how you want to come into the world, how you want to affect it.

And interestingly enough, matter moves in the same patterns as the emotions. When you look at how water swirls, like currents in the ocean, you see that air moves in the exact same pattern.

Looking closer at this you also see how everything in existence is formed with the same spinning motion, but with a different time perspective. From the strands of DNA to the largest mountains, all the way out to galaxies, all formed with the same spinning motion, all appearing and disappearing over time.

You also affect your own physicality and your whole being when you take care of your water needs or when you neglect it. As you find your inner peace of mind - when you stop stressing, worrying, judging or aggressively approaching life - you create a more healing environment, both inside of you and in your external reality.

Stress and trauma.

Think of stress in your body much like contracting a muscle. Lifting a heavy weight puts the muscle under stress. In this state nothing flows naturally or easy. This goes for your entire organism. When you expose it to stress, be it emotional or physical, you create contractions and stasis, stopping the flow of energy, water and blood through your system. The same phenomenon happens when you go through a painful, traumatic experience.

The event that caused the trauma, let's say a partner breaks up with you, you are attacked, bullied or you are in a car accident, brings up unhealed memories of previous events from your childhood which now makes themselves known with the same force as when they took place.

The old wounds that are reopened by the breakup/ bullying/attack or car accident impacts you with the same intensity as when the original trauma took place.

So if you felt abandoned as a child but you managed to get past it and grow up, you most likely still have a charge or contraction around certain occurrences or behaviors, and you act out in anger or fear so you will not feel the painful experiences from your childhood. This often happens subconsciously and you don't even know why you don't like certain behaviors or experiences.

The energetic charges and triggers you have around specific behaviors or happenings make you like a magnet for those particular behaviors. So if you are of the jealous kind due to traumatic experiences in your childhood, the charge and contraction around a certain behavior keeps you on the lookout for it, thereby attracting more of it into your life and you are forced to relive the same trauma over and over, until you heal it and let it go.

The process of healing the trauma will be discuss towards the end of this book. When you let go of your mind and go with the flow you allow Life to unfold for you, you become part of the flow of life itself. Thus you let the energy of evolution, much akin to a river, take you and show you the way.

You are part of the wave of energy that is Life evolving into Being itself. You are co-creating the course of Life and when you align your personal intention with that of the Dream of the Planet you fall into flow.

To be a co-creator in Life means that you align your will and your energy with that of Life itself. You step into your whole Self and become aware of the many ways Ego and fear manifests in your life. Because now you know that you are Life.

The Ego believes in separation and the fear-based, "not enough-ness" of your mind, while your Soul knows that Nature is everlasting. The river does not worry about if it will return next year. It lives in the Knowing, in presence of the eternal nature of our world, our Universe, of which you are also a beautiful part — never separate from — always a part of. In short, you let Life flow the way the river flows to the ocean, knowing that it is all coming together at the end.

The never ending cycle of water, first being in a fluid state, then evaporating into the atmosphere, then coming back to earth as rain, shows us much of our own cycle of energetic reincarnation on our planet.

You appear as an expression of the eternal flow of energy in our world and as you live you either fill the universe with more love and a higher vibration or you live in fear and you become a taker, adding to the myth of lack and separation.

When you awaken to your true nature you learn deeply that there is no separation in the quantum field of energy, that your true inner blueprint, your energy body and the whole chakra system, return to its original form as your physical body dissolves.

To learn to trust life, the process of existence, and to let go of control, is to learn the lessons contained in Water, to Be Water. You let go of ego and join the current of Life when you go with the flow of never-ending possibilities.

I Am Earth

2. You Are Earth

How on Earth are you Earth? The old adage "from dust to dust" reminds you that you are made of particles from our Earth Mother, the soil itself. Your actual physical body consists of the same building material as Earth Mother herself. How is this even possible? That's what this chapter is about.

The healing powers contained in our original environment is vast and completely forgotten in our modern society. You ground your energy system with Earth Mother's energy when you connect with Her through walks, hikes, baths in the ocean or lakes, or in meditation.

Humans have lived in the energy field of Earth Mother for our whole existence, and until the last few hundred years, we were aware of this connection and the need to keep it healthy and sacred as She, Earth Mother, kept us safe. We had developed and we maintained a relationship with our home planet. Not so anymore.

Physically Speaking

Our modern city living have separated us from a natural way of life. We no longer live in houses built from timber or find dwelling in caves or teepees. Instead we find ourselves in modern houses and buildings made with concrete, chemically created, heavy metal laden paints, plastics, drywall, and other artificial materials.

These building materials have a different energetic imprint than that of the natural materials we previously used for homes. The modern construction materials create an immense disconnection from our original state. Energetically speaking this creates different forms of disease and dissonance.

What do I mean by this?

Here's an example. Walk into a modern concrete office building and notice how you feel in your

energy field and in your body when you are there.
Do you feel tired, maybe heavy, or do you get a
slight headache? Maybe it is a little harder to
breathe and feel comfortable.

Now go into an older log cabin or a wooden house
and feel how your energy feels. Does it feel the same
as in the concrete building or different? Do you
notice any difference?

When you begin to listen to how you actually feel in
different situations and how your body
communicates with you, you will develop your
skills in interpreting what feels right and healthy or
when your body tells you something different.

Your body and every organ has an innate wisdom
and if you want to live healthier lives you need to
learn how to listen to it.

Modern day zoos.

Rocks are broken down mountains, as is sand and
parts of the soil. Your nature is to live in contact
with these substances and to experience the
energetic exchanges that happen when you spend
time in your natural environment.

If you take a fish out of its ordinary environment
and put it in a fishbowl with a different pH level,
the fish will most likely not survive, and if it does, it

gets sickly and weak. With this in mind it is easy to see that we have built ourselves into a modern day zoo.

Humans' natural habitat is the forest, the mountains and the ocean, not the city. If you doubt my words, spend a few days in nature and see how different this makes you feel. And much like the poor sickly animals trapped in cages for our entertainment, we develop a plethora of diseases connected to our modern day lifestyle, just like the fish that gets sick in the different pH level water.

We have created a very acidic environment, both internally in our bodies, and externally in the environment, by using pesticides on the crops, chemicals to purify our water, and the pollution from all the exhaust of oil based fuels from the car-, airplane- and boat industry. The doctor recommends to reconnect with our original habitat in order to create healing, as well as cleaning up our home, our Earth Mother.

An interesting point of view is to look at Earth Mother as a home, as our home. Imagine if you come home to your friend or your child and their home is filled with toxic waste and trash everywhere. You would get upset with them and convince them to clean up. You would most surely tell them how unhealthy it is to live in such unsanitary conditions. Well, it's not much different when take an honest look at how we treat our home, Earth, is it?

We are one of many carbon-based life forms on Earth. We are molecularly made up of carbon, which also makes up a large part of our planet. The soil which our food is grown in is made of eroded rocks and decomposed organic matter; trees, plants and bodies.

Rocks, sand and soil were once mountains that over a long period of time have become what they are today. Erosion, created by weathering, have broken larger pieces of rocks into smaller and smaller fragments until it becomes sand.

The trace elements, minerals and particles that make up the rocks are the same elements needed in the soil for the plants and crops to thrive and be healthy.

These minerals and trace elements are the same you need in order to stay strong and well. Your vitamins and supplements consist of the same minerals that the plants need. In essence, you consist of the same matter as Earth Mother herself. You are Earth Mother in a different form.

You take vitamins and minerals made in the soil, consisting of the same elements that the plants live from, which in extension, are the same of which animals live. And you live either of the plants or the animals. So you are made up of exactly the matter of the soil.

We are like cells on Earth Mother.

From one perspective, humans on planet Earth, can be likened to cells or bacteria on your own body. When you take a closer look at your own body you realize that you are made up of many small parts, bacteria and cells. As these parts interact, they create your body. Can you separate a single cell or a bacteria from the whole of your body, or are they intrinsically connected?

If you zoom out into space you see that planet Earth is also made up of both trees, plants, animals and humans. You are part of the living system known as Earth Mother or Earth.

Mountains and nature itself are full of negative ions, whose benefits I in the chapter on water. This is one of the reasons you feel so much better when you spend time in nature, around waterfalls, in the mountains or woods, or by the ocean. This is the reconnection you so desperately desire when you live in modern buildings and cities.

And the reconnection, be it energetic or physical in nature, is one of the many ways our planet communicates with you. The flow of negative ions have a huge impact on your wellbeing and health.

Surrounding Earth Mother is an electromagnetic field, the magnetosphere, created by the iron ore in the core of the planet. This field protects you from harmful radiation from the sun and from space as well as it connects every living thing on your planet. You live in this electromagnetic field as well as you are electromagnetic in your own nature.

Everything in existence, from the coffeecup in your hand, to the rock outside the window, to your own body, has spinning atoms that create physical bodies and objects. The spin of these atoms create the electromagnetic field, which you can affect and measure with your intentions and your actions.

This is part of how you are connected both to Earth Mother and other people. When you break down what thoughts are you see that they are electric charges in your brain, and in your energy field.

These charges carry energy which resonate through your energy field and reverberate through the magnetic field, through the field of consciousness.

This is why when you think of someone, they call you a minute later. Or how you can feel when something is about to happen or when someone is thinking of you. We are intrinsically connected through the magnetic field and other frequencies of our Earth Mother.

You Are Earth Mother.

Spiritually Speaking

You are an expression of the Consciousness that is Life, and Life's innate desire to create more Life.

Think of it this way.

The manifestation of Life is like an energetic ripple across our globe. This flow of creation is much like a tidal wave that creates through the fabric of existence. When you pour enough water on a surface it will spread and cover that surface. The same principle goes for the energy of Life. Life has taken different forms throughout the ages, moss and lichens became plants and then evolved, becoming separate beings, such as dinosaurs and other creatures.

Different factors of survival and habitats changed on our planet and life changed with it; over time humans evolved as a result of the trial and error of

The mayfly lives for only one day as an adult insect and from the mayfly's point of view, humans live forever and the mayfly may have no understanding or insight into the life and death of a human, since the mayfly knows only one day of existence.

The same concept goes for humans living on earth. We cannot grasp the vast existence of millions and billions of years. Another way of looking at this; we know that our bodies are made up of trillions of cells. The cells on your left hand may not have any idea that there are cells just like them on the right hand, or on the foot.

Each one of the cells may not be aware about the whole of the body, that the body is a living, breathing organism. Each cell may only know of its own existence.

When we zoom out on earth we realize that humans are much like the cells in our body, or like ants in the forest, without any real clue that we are part of the whole of Earth Mother, that She is a living, breathing organism.

From "Dust to Dust".

We complete the cycle of life, as our bodies compose into Earth itself, the same process as when rocks erode and become soil. The carbon molecules in the ground are the building blocks for our bodies and when we die we disintegrate back into earth, either we are cremated or buried, and our molecules recycle into earth.

Our connection to Earth Mother is such: we live in her energetic field and are dependent on the ions, minerals, nutrients and magnetic force which she bestows upon us.

Our Earth Mother is surrounded by an electromagnetic field — created by the sheer mass of the globe— and by the life force on the Planet, as well as the biodynamic field of Intentionality created by Life's desire for itself. You live within that field of Intentionality.

The Intention for Life is to create more Life, until it understands itself. This is where your higher understanding comes into play. This is why you are here. To be a reflection of Creation itself.

We are the answer to Life's desire for more Life, but we have misunderstood the function of this and many of us grab, live in fear and pollute as a result of this fear-based misunderstanding.

Page 30

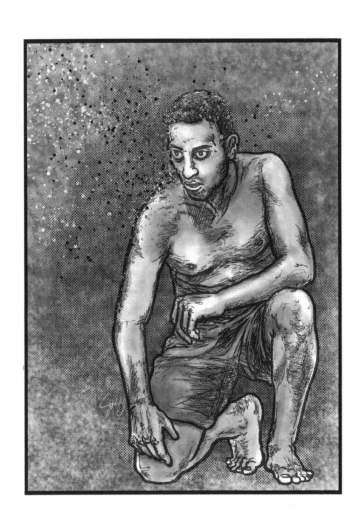

I Am Air

3. You Are Air

The element of Air, also known as Wind, is fundamentally interconnected with your whole existence. Think about it and you realize that every cell in your body is dependent on oxygen for survival, that every actual breath means the difference between life and death. Your breath is so deeply entwined with your existence that it is with you from the first moment of birth until your last breath - the final transition out of this physical dimension.

Physically Speaking

You inhale life-giving oxygen, O2, which is absorbed into the alveoli in your lungs and transported via the bloodstream to every part of your body. Breath is the vehicle for Life energy to enter your physical being.

Your body is made up of cells that all cooperate, somewhat like independent contractors working for one large corporation, overseen by the larger Consciousness of You, which in turn is connected to Source i.e. the large electromagnetic field of Earth Mother. This is how we all connect.

And also how you connect with all different forms of energy that exist in the field of consciousness. Life as we know it, originated from prokaryotic cells (original cells without an internal cell structure) in the oceans millions of years ago (or so we believe). Over time these cells organized into structures of organs and protective layers, guided by the desire of Life to evolve.

These organic structures, guided by the higher intelligence of Life force itself, took the form of carbon based life forms, as Life learned about itself. This is how we get what we call evolution.

Small groups of cells organized themselves into larger groups that needed an outer layer to protect themselves, subsequently creating an outer layer of skin or hide. Oxygen needed to be transported through the skin into the inner workings of the new organism. So different forms of lungs or gills were created, becoming membranes allowing oxygen to flow into the new being.

Again, this way life learned from its own development. With each organ having an awareness of itself through cells entraining with each other and developing intelligence, the larger organism also developed an awareness and consciousness of itself.

Life is striving to fulfill its desire to become complete in the physical through different forms, the current form being humans and the rest of the animal and plant world. The formation of Creation is fascinating — so deep and vast —that it is almost impossible for us to grasp.

When you grow in conscious awareness of your breath you also grow deeper into your "beingness", and learn to listen inward. You discern what each breath tells you as you get more in touch with yourself.

Notice when you feel low, if you feel oppressed or emotionally abused, how this brings about a feeling of being unworthy. Your breathing becomes more and more shallow as your body contracts to protect itself from either the oppressive and bullying energy or from the inner pressure you experience.

This is a response to emotional trauma and now your body physically protects itself from those unpleasant feelings. Your vital blood flow and lymph get restricted and slowly your physical body starts to take damage. This leads to inflammation and over time to different chronic illnesses and conditions.

When you look at yourself or a friend who was bullied in school you can quickly see how the physical posture of the person, or yourself, changed to protect from more bullying.

When you are self-conscious about a specific part of your body you may try to hide that part, or protect it. Over time this affects your posture, resulting in misalignment of the joints and bones, which over time causes both inflammation and serious injuries. In this process you will believe that you were just not built "right", which is what western medicine says. Unfortunately western medicine is not aware of underlying conditions the way shamans look at health and body and mind.

Most of western medicine is looking at the symptom of a condition, such as a misaligned back, as the problem. They don't see that the underlying reason is emotional and energetic in its origin and that the cure for the disease can also be found there.

If you manage to treat the inflammation but you don't clear the energetic imprint of the hurt or unworthiness, which is the original cause of this condition, the inflammation and condition will return within a short amount of time.

Cellular Intelligence.

With each new breath of life we create healing on a cellular level. This whole process is, of course, involuntary, and completely perfected by the innate intelligence of your body.

The energetic imprint, i.e., blueprint for the body, is already present before the physical form, and this blueprint leads the way for the physical body to constantly improve itself. This is the intelligence contained in every cell, as the cells become entrained with another.

What is Entrainment?

Entrainment is when any body of matter or energy, be it a cell or a human, or even celestial body, adjusts itself to the vibratory signature of its surrounding bodies.

It may be easier to see it as harmony of strings. When one string vibrate in tune the sound comes out clear and beautiful, but when it is out of tune the resulting sound is in discord or out of tune. And when several strings are strummed at the same time they vibrate together and adjust to the overall vibration of the whole, creating a beautiful symphony.

This also happens in humans, animals, cells, or any kind of vibratory movement of any particles or bodies.

It often occurs when humans spend time together: women having synchronized monthly menstrual cycles , choirs singing in harmony, groups of individuals sharing similar feelings. Or when pendulums swing and begin to harmonize after a certain amount of swings. The waves in the ocean align the same way.

The Dutch physicist Christian Huygens discovered this principle when he realized that the pendulums on the clocks on his wall suddenly synchronized with each other. If you do further research on entrainment you find that it is the universal principle behind many of our phenomena in the natural world.

Entrainment also happens when cells group together, as within your heart. The cells of the heart develop their own unique intelligence through the unison vibration they adjust to, just like the brain. The cells in a body align to a preexisting blueprint which is what we refer to as consciousness. Intelligence transpires when cells or groups organize and entrain with one another.

The famous botanist Stephen Harrod Buhner writes beautifully about the phenomenon of entrainment in the heart in his 1996 book "Sacred Plant Medicine".

We also see this in gang fights, in group demonstrations, in political rallies or in other settings where several individuals are gathered and act as one large organism.

Often we see at concerts all the bodies moving together in unison, based on the music, but nevertheless, they act like one organism, in rhythm and entrainment.

Here's a test you can do. When you are in a crowd of people, whistle a tune. Do it for a little bit. Within a few moments or minutes you will other people whistle. They may not even be aware that they heard you whistle, they just got the feeling to whistle, but it was prompted by your whistling. Or if someone is singing and it evokes a feeling in the whole crowd. Watch a street musician play a certain well known song, be it sad or upbeat, and observe how the whole crowd is struck by the same feeling.

Or just go and observe a concert. When the song comes on that makes everyone swing in unison, when everyone jumps together, they are entrained to the rhythm of that particular vibration. This is entrainment.

Entrainment causes consciousness to reason and to make judgment calls for survival.

Your heart responds to an emotional or physical loss. The heart reacts to a separation from another heart, which it is entrained with, almost like death. This explains why so many people either can't get over an ex-lover or why people may die from a broken heart. The separation truly affects the physical and energetic structure of the heart.

And when it comes to heartbreak there's more. Once two people and their hearts have become entrained with each other in the specific frequency of their hearts, they are forever connected through the energy field of our planet.

This is the same phenomenon as when quantum physicists discuss quantum entanglement, which means that when two particles have been part of the same vibration, entrained on each other, they are connected outside of time and space. In experiments quantum physicists have been able to prove that once the two cells have become entrained in the same frequency or vibration, they can be separated all the way out to space and what the physicists do to one particle also happens to the other particle, whether it be separated by thousands of miles or not.

The cells that are entrained with each other, as in in the heart or other organs, react innately and with their own instinctive awareness to save the whole being.

In other words, there are several centers in your body with their own innate intelligence that guide and direct your life in ways that the conscious part of your brain doesn't really understand. In fact, every organ has its own intelligence due to entrainment.

Patterns of the Mind.

The brain and the mind can only understand the world in retrospect, by looking at the past to decide the future actions, which is why you often get stuck in patterns that are unhealthy for you.

The brain doesn't know how to live without fear, without looking backwards, so the brain is always judging the present moment based on past experiences, which usually recreates more of the same type of experiences.

Here is a simplified example: If you run into a bear when you leave your cave home and go left, you learn that there is a bear to the left so you determine that it is safer to go right or straight ahead. The next day you turn right and to your surprise you run into a pack of coyotes. Now your brain learns that it is unsafe to go right as well. So the third time you leave the cave you decide to go straight ahead. And guess what, this time you run into an enemy tribe. By now your brain has learned that it is unsafe to leave the cave at all.

So you decide to stay in the safety of your cave. But in reality, the bear, the coyotes and the enemy tribe have all left and moved on, while you are still stuck in the fear you experienced before.

This may sound farfetched but is it really? If you replace the animals and the enemy with the last few relationships you've had, or the way you grew up, it is easy to see that your mind keep the fears alive by being on a sort of repeat.

When a trauma has become stuck in our system the feeling of the trauma triggers a thought of fear, which in turn triggers the feeling even deeper. This is how you unknowingly keep the fears in your system alive.

Your fears are there to keep you safe, but they are often mistaken, either based in other people's opinions and beliefs or in experiences of the past, not now.

In this moment you are totally and completely free. But not as long as you let your fears get the best of you. It is only when you open up your mind, when you learn to live in the flow of the present moment, which can only be perceived and understood by the heart or the gut, that you find true happiness.

A brain free from inner distractions functions on a much higher level of capacity than one that is constantly sidetracked.

Reflecting upon how bodies (human and mammal) are formed, we see that it takes an intelligence far beyond our own to create the structures needed to supply all the life-supporting elements.

Entrainment, and the high vibration of Love — coherence, compassion, tolerance and understanding — is the only solution for Life to thrive as this is the one vibration that is creative and sustainable. When you think about it, where does destruction lead us?

If the cells of life or the energy of the sun was not a creative force, would any of our world exist today? An eye for an eye makes the world go blind. The same goes for a destructive force in the universe. If our world was not made up of the creative, upwards spiraling force of love the world would not exist today. Life itself is a creative, up-building force.

When we align our intention and energy with that truth, we shift our consciousness into alignment with that of Earth Mother and Life itself.

But the same can also be said for negative vibrations. When many of us align with negativity or resonate with anger and judgment, we create destruction. This is what makes up evil.

So we do what we can to align with the higher vibration of Love and Compassion, since these are creative and upbuilding in energy.

Spiritually Speaking

Through the element of Air you can connect with others using your intention.

Humans are living bundles of energy; we actually live in a sea of energy. You are surrounded by the element of air, comprised of nitrogen, oxygen and other gases. The atmosphere is full of molecules of nitrogen and oxygen, which all carry a charge. You live in the midst of that charge and communicate through it and through other fields of energy.

The electromagnetic field surrounding Earth Mother makes this possible. You influence this field with your energy and intention and you are impacted by others as well.

When you raise the individual frequency of your personal energy field, aura or bio magnetic field, you also impact the field around you and raise the collective vibration in which you live.

When you dip a heating rod into a cold lake the heat causes the molecules closest to the hot rod to begin to move faster and faster, making the molecules around them also move faster. This is how heat spreads in water.

And just like that lake, you influence the field around you. When you are in your higher vibration this reverberates through the energy around you and it has an impact on others.

Breath and Trauma.

Air is Life for humans. When you go through a traumatic experience your body responds by tightening up. That way the trauma gets stuck in your body and often you forget to breathe.

As a result of the unhealed trauma you often develop chronic physical problems due to the constrained flow of both blood, oxygen and energy in your body. Your breath and your life are intrinsically connected.

The yogic tradition of Pranayama addresses the many ways in which your breathe is connected to help you deal with trauma and emotional problems.

There are many different breathing techniques in yoga, all of them with different impact on your system.

Energizing your body with the help of the breath is an amazing healing experience, reaching depths that only deep meditation and serious energy work can. This also points to the connection between your breath and your emotional state.

Learning to breathe properly can make a difference in how you feel and profoundly change your emotional state.

People who suffer from anxiety often feel like they can't breathe; when they finally take a proper, deep breath, the physical relaxation in their body is remarkable. Notice how your body and breath reacts when you think of something fearful.

Learning how to clear your throat chakra — how to deepen your breath through yogic breathing techniques and connect your mind to your Heart — helps us keep the oxygen flowing in your body and how to stay connected to it.

And spiritually speaking, air teaches us transparency and honesty, traits quite forgotten in our modern world. More about this in the chapter on implementing Air.

I Am Fire

4. You Are Fire

Humans consist of matter, which in its deepest form is energy. Einstein said that all matter is light in vibration. So even when we look at our bodies we realize that on the deepest level we are Light, which is fire.

And the way electrical impulses move through our nerves is yet another form of fire. When we break it down we see that the carbon in our bodies once was the same carbon in Earth, that the Air we breathe is how the cells in our bodies get their energy, and how Water helps both purify us and keep us alive.

The fourth element of Fire can also be viewed as electricity in our bodies. We pay much attention to our physical bodies but most of us seem unaware that we are primarily made of energy.

We go to the gym, work out, hike, and are careful with what we put into our physical bodies. But are we working on our energy bodies? What do we do to take care of our energetic body, our energy? We are more concerned with our"six-packs" — the size of our biceps and waists — than we are of our inner peace, mental clarity, and awareness.

Physically Speaking

You are Fire. Consider the flow of electric currents that constantly runs through your body. This flow of energy carries messages between all of your different organs and body parts - telling the heart when to beat and the lungs when to inhale/exhale. It also communicates between our organs to release toxins and other residual materials from our system. These messages through your body makes it possible for you to feel and understand your body.

If you doubt your inner fire, just think of a time when you have been extremely angry or furious. You can certainly feel that fire in your belly.

And if you have ever truly been in Love you know the power of that fire in your soul. The energizing effect in your body, the spark in your heart and stomach, is a sign of high activity on a cellular level. Your system is on fire and you can feel it.

In some ways this is your body's way of preparing for creating more life. When the body feels the connection to that other person, your body gets ready to support more life so it gets energized. This is one of those good signs for a healthy relationship.

And vice versa, when your body shuts down you know this is also a sign.

DNA and Light.

Looking deep into our physical bodies we see that also our DNA uses light to communicate.

Researchers studied DNA chromosomes under fluorescent light and discovered that strands of DNA light up and produce their own light, activating the messaging contained within the DNA*[4].

This is the process of the DNA that informs which proteins will be activated in new cells, thereby creating a blueprint for the cells. Our bodies use light on a cellular and molecular level to communicate*[5].

Our Western, scientific point of view, finds us lacking in the understanding of the many ancient spiritual traditions.

Indian sages and Chinese medicine, as well as South American and North American Shamans, have long worked with the Energy Body. They discovered that the energy field surrounding your body is as real as your own flesh and bones.

By healing your energy bodies, you are in fact healing your physical body. We on the Shamanic path believe that the blueprint for your physical body can be found in your energy body.

Fire and Evolution.

Fire meant life for human kind. When we learned to harness the power of fire, and the lessons we learned from it, we took a big leap in our evolution.

We learned to cook our food, we discovered how to stay warm and survive in climates that were inhabitable before.

By cooking our food we released nutrients that were more easily accessible for our system and we also extended our life span. The discovery of harnessing fire gave us a sense of security and of power in life.

Consider the immense evolution that took place after we began to use fire purposefully. From the early cave man days fire was necessary for survival, securing food and making tools, and then we learned how to control it and we created motion with it. We created the steam engine, driven by fire heating up water in order to make propulsion.

Look at the origin of how we used fire, first we just stayed warm, then we heated food, and we began to use if to make pottery and tools. This resulted in the discovery of making kilns and creating steel tools and weapons.

Over time the kiln led someone to realize the inherent power in using heat for power exchange.

And slowly the origins of the steam engine grew within the conscious mind of humans.

When we learned to create motion with heat and fire, we took the first steps towards creating electricity. Then we learned more about the power of electricity, but we would never have reached that conclusion if it wasn't for the use of fire.

When we look at how we have learned to control fire and make it into a useful element in our world we see that from what used to be fire, we created electricity.

This thought gave birth to the use of electricity and the spool of magnetism, which is how we harness the power of electricity. See what electricity has created in our modern day society. Everything is based in electricity, from cars to computers. Our banking, our entertainment, our travel, is all based in electricity.

Sure, we are using different modes of fuel, such as petroleum and other sources, but without the electrical spark we would have no transportation or communication.

This was fire and came to make up the backbone of all of our modern world.

So just like Fire likened to electricity in our bodies is how the body communicates between cells and organs, so do we also communicate across our globe with the use of electrical impulses, across the internet, the phones and other modes of communication.

Humans are Fire.

The nature of Fire is change. Fire takes one element and turns it into another form, say wood into gaseous carbon molecules. Or look at ice melted into water from the heat of fire, or when water turns gaseous.

From that point of view, we humans are like Fire ravaging across Earth. We take materials and change them into new materials, as well as pollute and burn our Earth home on which we live.

Humans are extremely capable of creating anything they intend to. We have to learn to create with intention of the highest good and for the healing of our world. There is immense power in fire, as well as there is within us, but we need to learn to use it wisely.

With great power comes great responsibility.

We can still learn how to create a healthy planet, by learning the ways of Nature, by allowing the flow of Life in nature to take its course, we can still be a part of this process.

To learn is to grow — to tap into a greater understanding of Life itself and a higher level of consciousness — free from the fear-based existence we've hitherto known.

Spiritually Speaking

To realize your deepest nature is to realize that you are energy. Who and what you truly are in your Heart is Energy. You can help this process by meditating and increasing your innerstanding (sic.) of yourself, reading spiritual books and by finding both a teacher and a group of like minded individuals. And of course, through increasing your connection with Earth Mother.

The Fire Element represents change. It represents passion. It represents the raging flames of Life itself. The force of Life is supremely strong; it endures all kinds of challenges and changes.

The connection you experience, if you have ever truly been in love, is that of Fire — a flame that consumes and changes you forever. If you are open to change and willing to grow, Fire is for you.

The passion that can be found in your heart and in your creativity is immense, and it is realized once you discover it in yourself. Creativity, passion, and all that you are become magnified when allowed to enter your consciousness.

When you sit down — be it to write your memoir or that screenplay you've been working on, color in a coloring book or paint — you are tapping into your deeper self and reaching your greatest potential. Make sure to stoke those embers of life so they glow and radiate, rekindling the Fire of Passion and Creativity that sustain you.

As you realize your own potential and come into alignment with your soul agreement, doors open inside of you that you never knew existed. You enter the creative flow of Life and you learn how to stay in it.

Personal Love and Fire Fire also represents personal Love and Procreation. Our human need to procreate is a manifestation of Life's own will — the Will for Life — for more if itself.

Think about it: Your sexual drive and desire are completely natural and bestowed upon you by the force called Life. When you feel the power of desire and love, you recognize the strength of Life's "want".

The biodynamic energy of Life - felt in you as desire and drive - is the core of yourselves and the driving engine for more life and more creativity.

On its deepest level Life is creativity. When cells divide into new cells - the flow of Life - they create more Life, just as humans procreate and make a new life. The same process, different scale and perspective.

Father Sun and Earth Mother.

The relationship between the Sun (Father) and the Earth (Mother) is another reflection of this expression.

When creating Life, Father Sun interacts with Mother Earth in much the same way as humans: A seed must be sown in order to create Life. At the moment the sperm cell of the human male meets the ovum of the female and the union results in a fertilized ovum (zygote), a new Life has begun.

And so it is with the Earth Mother and Father Sun. A seed is planted in the soil/Mother Earth and is fortified by the light/love of the sun/Father Sun. The true fabrication of Life, however, takes place within the Mother. This is the Fire of Life within Earth Mother, kindled by Father Sun. It is all connected.

5. Implementing Water

You Are Water.

Heart Chakra, Movement, Life, Flow, Acceptance. What does this mean for you and me? How do we apply this in our every day life in order to grow as humans?

Water, by nature, is supple. Water has tremendous force but is also soft and fluid. The wise teachings of martial arts tell us that to be water means to be fluid — to be mendable and pliable — and allow Life itself to flow. To be Water you must be consistent and persistent, accepting whatever comes your way.

Water has the power, over time, to erode and move mountains and change a landscape. When applying this process to our own lives, we understand that we must be patient; we need to accept the process as we learn to be more tolerant of ourselves and our world, as well as knowing that the power of consistency will shape our lives.

Consider the practice of Tai Chi; how they mimic the energy and force of water. Tai Chi is at first sight a slow and mindful practice with no practical application as self defense. But watch a Tai Chi master perform the movements in rapid speed and you will see astonishing fighting results of a martial arts that at first appears to be only peaceful and meditative.

The Ocean (Water) is an all-encompassing and persuasive teacher. Watching her, we learn to appreciate the very essence of movement. She embodies the nature of all things in motion — every atom spinning and rotating - and brings us home to ourselves: the cyclical nature of Life, a deeper sense of Self and true Oneness.

Water also shows you how to Love like the Ocean. The Ocean doesn't carry any judgment or separation, but only is Love.

So when you are in Love, be like the Ocean, steadfast and faithful in your Love. There is a beautiful is-ness to the Ocean, a sense of pure existence and beingness. The Ocean shows you how to be detached and become like Water.

Below the Surface.

Watching the Ocean during a storm, you tend to see only raging waters: the waves and wind tear at the surface creating a huge swell. But, if you dive only a few feet below the surface, there is stillness.

The deeper you go into the Ocean of the mind and into the stillness, the more you discover the deeper aspects of yourself and the silence that can be found here.

This is how you do it. When you experience feelings and triggers such as anger, anxiety, happiness, rage, or regret, and go deeper within yourself, you understand that these are only "surface" emotions. You need to still yourself long enough to sit in meditation and reach deep down, beyond the "surface" of your opinions and judgments. It is there, in the depth of yourself that you discover your True Being, your true nature beyond your mind's programming. Often this programming is full of triggers that start your emotional rollercoasters.

Water also teaches us the Oneness of all things — our interrelationship with Nature. Fish swimming in the ocean, as well as many life forms found there, are all connected by water, bound by the same Energy.

This is the same energy that connects humans with other life forms on Earth. We seldom think of Air being just another form of Water but they are similar in structure, with air being of a lesser density. When we grasp this we understand that there is a connection between us and every other living being on Earth.

Meditation

Sit or lie in your favorite meditation pose. Take a few deep breaths. Feel the oxygen fill every cell of your body.

Slow your mind.

Drop your mind into your Heart.

As your mind begins to focus on the heart center, envision yourself at the bottom of a deep ocean.

Watch yourself sitting in the deep blue green water mass.

Feel the water on your skin, the deep, vast silence of the Ocean.

Sit with it.

Then a fish swims by, you observe it, and you let it to move on. Next a large whale swims by, this catches your attention, but as you sit there you learn that the whale too, just keeps swimming by.

Your thoughts are like fish and other creatures swimming by in the vastness of the ocean; they come to you in the depth of your stillness.

When you anchor yourself into Being, you'll notice these thoughts — maybe even identify them — but then be able to let them go without attaching meaning to them.

If a shark "thought" appears, just let it pass as you would any other fear.

Allow the thoughts to flow by you, without attaching a story to them.

Feel the feeling, but let go of the story.

Sit in the Stillness and Beingness of the Ocean.

Become the Ocean, Be Water.

6. Implementing Air

You are Air

Crown chakra, Third Eye, Throat, Life, Breath, Wind, Dance. Air is the source of all human life forms. Everything about us humans is connected to oxygen, aka Air.

As stated, every cell in your body needs oxygen to function.

To implement aspects of Air into your spiritual life, sit with it, preferably in nature, maybe on a mountaintop or on a hill somewhere and observe it. The element of Air is completely transparent. You see straight through it and you barely feel it unless there is a breeze or temperature change. Air is very much present in your life without you ever thinking much about it.

When you sit with Air you realize that this is honesty and transparency.

That this is how you can learn to live your life without fear.

When you learn to be real with your feelings and own your own inner space, you also learn the importance of honesty. It creates a sense of integrity and power in your life.

A power so many have given away to outer circumstances, such as social media, family members, people pleasing, virtually everything that makes you feel bad or powerless.

Air - Honesty, Transparency.

As you become the experience of Air things become clear.

The process can look like this: washed by Water, cleared and released into Air. The saying "hung out to dry" means that our dirty laundry is out in the open.

Air teaches honesty and transparency; it becomes the foundation of the ethics of our lives. When we learn to truly "see" through Air we begin to pick up on the subtle nuances of energy, of intuitive seeing and knowing.

This way we become familiar with transparency. Transparency and honesty exist in the same realm and are at times synonymous.

Honesty is a derivative of the word honor. Honor means "high respect, great esteem" or "regard with great respect" or "to fulfill an agreement".

So when you honor yourself you hold yourself in high regard, you carry yourself with great respect, or you fulfill your agreements with yourself. Do you see how beneficial this is?

When we live with honor, we live with honesty and transparency and we become integral, as in fully integrated with ourselves.

There is no longer a discrepancy between your inner self and your outward actions. You mean what you say and you are who you say you are.

This is a beautiful state of existence, far underestimated today.

Implementing Air into your life guides you into a state of honor and honesty.

Air allows you to see both into yourself and into the world of the unseen. The lesson of the unseen starts with Water, revealing worlds you cannot see until you immerse yourself in it.

It then continues with the world of Air, which is translucent and yet still hides the finer workings of energy from your eyes.

What I mean is that the airwaves are filled with fields of radiation and energy, made up of electricity, magnetism, gravity, energy and more.

All of these are unseen by your eyes, but they still exist, much like if you are living a lie, the truth is still there, just hidden from people's perception.

In order to reach true freedom, you must learn to be honest and transparent, both with yourself and others. This is necessary for any kind of real Freedom.

This is what Air teaches you - to be real with yourself and others. If you are not happy in a situation, you need to be clear with yourself and your intentions — to know your own wants and desires.

By doing so you become fully aligned with who and what you truly are and your purpose in this particular lifetime.

Trauma and Chronic Illness.

When you experience discord between your original vibration — in its purest form from childhood — and the life you live, this discord will manifest itself as different emotional maladjustments.

Usually it is the trauma may you have experienced that causes this dissonance or discord in your system.

And it is also the trauma the becomes the underlying origins for both emotional and physical disease. As this feeling becomes part of how you see yourself and your relationship to the external world, you develop different issues, such as worry, anxiety, low self worth or self esteem, etc., all boiling down to a sense of discord.

Your emotional state, affected by the original discord and disassociation you experience, influence how you carry yourself physically. This in turn creates a recycling of experience and emotions, all of which cements your belief about yourself or the world as a whole.

If a feeling of not being worthy is present in your system, you may experience discomfort in and around your stomach, solar plexus or butt.

When you feel a certain way you develop contractions in certain muscles as well as the fascia stiffens up in those areas (fascia = a layer of tissue underneath your skin keeping muscles and soft tissue in place), leading in turn to physical ailments.

When you constantly walk around with that pit in your stomach/solar plexus/butt you tense up the muscles in the area, changing your body's posture, maybe pushing the lower back out of alignment, which in turn leads to a weak back, pain in your stomach or a misaligned pelvis.

These misalignments cause physical pain, leading over time to conditions which modern medicine recognizes as chronic and treat with medication. The medication works as a band-aid for the conditions which originates in your emotional/spiritual/energetic self.

By not treating the original issue we never find true solace and the conditions keep worsening.

Another way of explaining this phenomenon is like this: Most of the chronic conditions in our modern world can be traced to an emotional and/or spiritual state of being. When you feel unworthy of either owning or expressing your emotions, you develop strategies to avoid feeling them. For example, if you are afraid that other people can be dangerous or that they pose a threat to you, you may walk in a defensive manner through life, shoulders up, hunching over a bit, always ready for an attack.

Or if you are afraid of conflict and constantly seek to please others, you may lower your head in an effort to seem submissive. What happens when you walk around in this posture, the submissive, people-pleasing style? People treat you accordingly to the subliminal messages you give out and you feel like the world is always treating you poorly and unfairly.

You may also have a difficult time expressing your truth, which leads to blockages in the throat chakra, or in the flow of energy in your throat.

The people pleasing, non-confrontational, hunched-over posture will lead both to neck problems as well as throat and thyroid problems, due to lack of circulation in those areas, both energetic and blood flow.

These postures cause contractions in your system, around certain organs and joints. The contraction gets stuck, both in your mental make up and in your fascia. When you experience a similar feeling or situation to the original trauma, your body contracts again and you react, often even stronger this time in order to feel safe. This causes a never-ending cycle of similar situations, based in your perception and emotional trauma. The constriction of energy flow also causes decay in the tissue and the blood flow to these organs, which lead to disease and illness.

As you heal these conditions you find that there are inflammations in the affected organs and joints that needs clearing.

But these will not be cleared unless you clear your energy body first.

This can be done both through deep meditation, energy healing work and bringing presence into our every day life and into our physical bodies.

The healing properties of Oxygen or Air, (or Wind), are many. As you meditate you learn to guide your breath to any area of your body that is either contracted, in pain or in need of healing. If a body part feels tight or contracted often a trigger hides here.

You can use this to investigate your triggers further. Trauma and emotional pain makes your body contract around the specific injury, whether it be emotional or physical.

The memory of the injury, stored both in your body and mind, keeps dictating your actions in order to not stir the trauma, so you don't have to relive it again.

This is how you unconsciously recreate the same tension and vibration in your system, keeping you on the look out for situations to avoid so you don't experience the pain again.

By always being in a state of fear, even when you don't know it or recognize it, you live in a state of vigilance. This state causes stress and you keep looking for the things and behaviors responsible for the pain, with the result that you will find what you look for, much like when you buy that new car and you suddenly see the same model everywhere.

Your body has a way of shielding you from pain but inadvertently it buries the pain deep inside of it instead, thereby creating triggers that are keeping the trauma in place. This creates contraction (tension and hardness) around certain body parts, be it your heart, lungs, stomach or other parts in your body.

Many women carry a lot of tension and pain in their hips, while men quite often carry theirs in their lower back.

How to find and identify trauma

in your body.

Sit in meditation pose, focus your mind into your body. Use your breath as a vehicle to bring your awareness into your body. Pay attention to where you have pain or where the breath feels stuck.

Now feel into your system, feel into your heart, feel into your stomach area, check in with your liver, your kidneys, your spleen and be alert to how your body responds. Is the pain in a certain part of your body, maybe in the knee or the liver? Or is there a slow, grinding pain in your stomach or lower abdomen?

When you feel the pain or contraction, watch what message or images come into your mind. Is the feeling connected to a memory or a specific person? Or a specific incident? It could be a physical or emotional event.

At first you are struck by the story connected with the feeling of the trauma. Bring yourself into this moment, knowing that the trauma happened before, not in this now.

Sit with the feeling of the trauma, face it, breath into it and just feel the emotional charge without the story connected to it.

For example, if you find a stabbing pain in your heart and you sit with that pain, you may realize that the pain is connected with a certain break up or experience with a partner.

Let's say that the feeling is abandonment or betrayal. Bring your awareness into the feeling and track where in your body the original feeling of abandonment or betrayal is located.

As you track the feeling there may be other memories coming up of similar emotional charge. When you reach the bottom of the feeling well, you will see that the original wound is connected to earlier experiences in your childhood.

Once you reach the original core wound you sit with that. The feeling that pops up can at first be difficult to accept and sit with, the first response may be to run away, to get distracted, like you have your whole life.

But when you can watch your core wound and sit with it, you allow it to be, create space for it and breathe into it, you let the body heal the wound from the inside out.

The body has an innate intelligence that knows how to heal wounds when you let it.

Here is a very powerful exercise in healing and reconnecting to your true self. With each breath create space around the area and breath into it. The practice allows the affected area to relax, to increase in blood flow, and thereby also exacerbate the healing process.

As you breathe in through your nose follow the oxygen to the trauma, sit with the feeling, visualize space around the organ or injury and observe the emotion connected to it.

Your body will tell you when you listen.

With each out-breath, release the energy which no longer serves you. You will find that there are many blockages you can remove and begin to heal this way.

A way to enhance the power in the above mentioned meditation technique is to use the vibration of the "Aum" chant.

The Aaaaa- part of the chant is focused on your stomach area and your intestinal area.

The uuuu- part focuses on your heart and lungs, as well as your throat, and finally the mmmm- part is focused on your brain and head.

So wherever your trauma or injury is stuck you focus the vibration of the sound into the trauma and allow the vibration to reverberate into the pained area.

Repeat the Aum for as long as needed, give yourself 30 minutes or more to do back to back Aums. Become the experience of the vibration and the Aum. These are the healing properties of Air and how to make use of them in your meditation practice.

Meditation

Meditate on Air.

Take in the life-giving energy and feel the oxygen reach every cell in your physical body; allow this to provide relaxation, safety and security for your body.

Feel the air molecules enter your nose, go down the back of your throat, into the wind pipes and finally reaches your lungs.

Experience the oxygen arrive at your Heart, and spread through your organism.

Follow the out breath, and as you become fully present in your body, watch the element of Air bring Honesty and Reality to you.

Honesty requires a certain kind of observation of yourself, an ability to see through your own thoughts and the inherent defenses you use to maintain your self-image.

When you sit with honesty in meditation you dismantle your thinking and you become the observer. This gives you a chance to realize when you are wrong or see a situation from a new perspective, instead of from your own limited place.

Air represents Willingness of movement.

You dance like the Air swirls and you find freedom.

This is the true essence of Air.

7. Implementing Earth

You are Earth

E arth, Mother, Heart, Grounded, Root Chakra. As you implement the element of Earth in your life, you reconnect and become one with Earth Mother herself.

This is a process of integrating into your heart, which leads to your root chakra, which in turn deepens the connection and rootedness into Earth

Mother herself. You become aware that you are held in the energy and love of Earth Mother, just like every living thing on our planet. Every single life form on Earth is part of the same energy field.

We are held and sustained by the energy of Life present on our planet and in the Universe. This means that it is the same spark of energy making your heart beat as in the calf, the dog, the cat, the bat, the eagle and the fish.

This driving force of energy is also behind the cells dividing in your body, and in that manner, also the same energy which drives plants to grow, every blade of grass and every tree to have cells dividing, creating more life.

You are Earth; your carbon-based life form was created from the molecules of Earth Mother. As you reconnect with Her, you discover a life force and wisdom that is inherent within you and thus become grounded — grounded in the connection to Earth Mother and a deeper sense of yourself. Like trees, whose root systems are secure in the place in which they belong, so too are you; you belong. Any feelings of loneliness and isolation fade away as you connect to Earth Mother and become your true self.

So in short, watch yourself grow roots into Earth Mother. You are loved, you are safe, now live accordingly.

Meditation

Version 1.

Make yourself comfortable, sitting or laying down. Take a few calming breaths. Find your center, and breathe into it. Give yourself a few minutes to slow down and come into your body.

For a few moments, pay attention to the energy in your body. Feel how your body feels, what is moving within your energy.

Move your attention to your root chakra, located at the tailbone, and imagine yourself growing roots, or shooting lightning bolts; thick, strong roots, into Earth Mother. Feel it happening. Sense the tingling sensation in the bottom of your spine as the roots get hold in Earth Mother and sit with that feeling.

When you feel grounded into Earth, move that energy up through your sacral chakra, located in the area of your navel.

Then allow the energy to pass up through your solar plexus chakra and into your heart. Sit with the flow of Earth Energy as it moves through your root chakra into your heart chakra.

Feel how you are being held in the energy of Mother Nature's loving and healing embrace.

Realize deeply that you are and always have been, held. You are as cherished and held as the trees, the grass, and all living entities on this beautiful planet we call Home.

Meditation

Version 2.

This meditation is best carried out in the outdoors. Find a park or better yet, a place in the mountains or by the ocean and do the meditation.

Sit by a tree, a lake or a mountain. Gather your thoughts, calm down and turn within.

Take in the smells, the feelings, the sounds and the energy of the area. After a few minutes you find yourself letting go of the external world of our society.

You find the regular stressors of life, the bills, phone calls, appointments, completely lose their importance when you take in Mother Nature and you become one with Her.

As you sit there let yourself go completely.

Transfer your consciousness into the lake or tree you are sitting by.

Imagine that you are the lake.

Become it, feel the water, feel the movement of the wind, the bird above you, the colors in the depth and the stillness that is the lake itself.

Experience pure existence without yourself.

Soon you realize that as the lake you have no story, no future, just pure existence in the moment.

You are the experience.

Stay there for as long as you want to/can. When you return to your body and yourself, give great thanks to the lake/tree/mountain you have just sat with and become.

8. Implementing Fire

You are Fire

Heart Chakra, Solar Plexus Chakra, Sacral Chakra, Root Chakra, Life, Light, Energy, Love, Passion, Creativity, Creation.

Fire is the great transformer; it turns your pain into pleasure and your pleasure into pain, until it teaches you the lesson of Being. When you "breathe into" your pain, you begin to learn how to face it. As you let go of the pain, it dissolves into the light of your Consciousness; it is transformed and becomes healing love.

Fire Ceremony

This is one version of a shamanic fire ceremony. Make sure that you are in a safe and sound space when you set up your fire.

There is a cleansing element to Fire; a fire ceremony is extremely healing and cleansing.

One way to make use of a fire ceremony is to set up your fire wood, prepare the area by burning sage and calling in the four direction in order to create sacred space.

You find a specific stick that stands out to you, that seem to call you. Take the stick and spend a few hours with it, holding it, carving messages into it, tying threads on it. For each thread or carving you infuse the wood with what it is you want to let go of. It can be a relationship, a character trait, a certain trauma or releasing karmic cycles.

You sit with the fire in meditation, you sit with the stick that you have infused with the energy you want to release and stare deeply into the flames.

Sit like that for as long as needed and you feel called to.

You can dance around the fire if you feel moved to do so and it is safe.

When you stare into the flames you will experience a lot of different states and possibly messages. Stay with it for as long as you feel is right and when you are ready put all the energy you want to release into the stick one last time and give it to the fire.

Watch it burn, feel the removal of the energies you need to let go of and watch them get consumed and transformed by the flames.

Stay with the fire until it goes out.

Then close out the sacred space with prayers of gratitude to the directions and to the spirit guides and power animals, as well as to the spirit of Fire.

Healing elements of Fire

The element of Fire is change. To apply this in your life you need the open mind of Air, the willingness of Water, and the groundedness of Earth.

You apply this willingness to change, to burn in the Fire of Awareness, to cleanse your past from your emotional and physical body, and you raise you vibration into your highest vibratory state.

When you learn how to breath into your blockages and contractions, when you face your pain and dissolve it in the light of your Consciousness you release and transform the energy trapped in the pain into healing light.

Consider performing the Fire Ceremony and become the flame as it dances through the cosmos. As you dance your way into the flames, ignite your passion for Life.

The fire of Life is all about passion and creativity! Creativity begins at conception and is the force of Life itself. Allow yourself to be creative and passionate; ignite the Fire of Life.

Become Life with the element of Fire. Scream, laugh, cry and dance yourself alive.

Fire is the element that brings new beginnings, clears the past, and transforms pain and suffering into gold.

Meditation

Version 1.

Fire Dance.

Either to be performed around a fire or anywhere you find fit. No physical fire is needed to perform this dancing meditation.

You can ask a good friend to drum, you can drum for yourself or play sacred drumming from any streaming platform.

First ask your guides to hold sacred space for you and enter into this space clearing yourself and your mind.

Feel the beat of the drum begin to move your body, first gently and slowly and then let it move you so you dissolve to the beat.

Become one with the drum and let yourself fly.

Feel the fire of creation in your belly clear you of all stagnant or negative energies.

Do this dance for as long as the drum keeps going or until you are finished.

Remember to close sacred space and to thank your allies for their support in your healing.

Version 2.

Prepare yourself for a calm, peaceful meditation on Life itself. Take a few deep breaths as you calm yourself into stillness. Drop your mind into your heart. Abide in the heart.

And now, watch the small ember of fire in your Heart. The ember catches on and becomes a flame. See this flame grow stronger, like a log catching on fire.

Let your inner fire spread throughout your chest, into your abdomen, up through your throat, and into the third eye chakra of your crown chakra. Allow the fire to flow down into the solar plexus, into the sacral chakra and your root.

Sit with the fire igniting all your chakras.

Watch the fire in your sacral chakra spin and grow; feel the heat build up inside of you. Allow this energy to spread out through your arms and your legs until it fills every part of you, every crevasse, every cell of your Being is now filled with the Fire of Existence, of Life itself.

Feel the invigorating power inherent in this flame.

Sit with it.

Allow it engulf you as you become the Fire.

You Are Fire.

Conclusion

T hank you for getting here. I am grateful you
did. I am grateful that just you are alive to
read these pages as you are a beautiful and
amazing expression of Life itself.

As the knowing contained in this book reaches more
hearts we will rise together. We are like a tide of
awareness sweeping across our world and it makes
me so excited and grateful that just you are here.

There are several reasons for becoming aware of
your connectedness with the elements.

As you learn the importance of your connection with the Elements and togetherness with Earth Mother, you become more fully human. Not only do you heal your core wounds but you also become a proponent of Earth Mother.

We come to understand that we, like all life on our planet, are loved and held in her precious energy. We are Earth. She is Us.

And look how cancer spreads in the body, first invading one organ, creating cancer there, then moving on to other organs via the pathways (lymph nodes or arteries) to other organs, slowly overtaking the whole organism.

Now zoom out on Earth Mother and look at how our cities and modern civilization looks. Isn't it eerily similar to how cancer invades and spreads through a body? Could it be that the way humans have evolved on Earth is much like a cancer?

And could it also be that we can still turn this ship around? That we can become benign and even beneficial for our Earth Mother?

There are so many ways we humans have destroyed our environment. We have ravaged our own Mother in the never-ending search for security.

The power struggles that we witness are all based in the primal fear of survival.

The good news is that the outward pollution and destruction is only a reflection of our inner state.

We have created a society that is so fear-ridden and disconnected from each other and our natural environment that we ourselves are getting sick as well as we sicken our Mother. This is good news because it means that there is a solution.

That solution is for each one of us to awaken to our inner health, our inner sense of who we are and our inner Love. Once we are in touch with ourselves, once we have found our way into our own heart and created a safe space in there, we will also have enough bandwidth and energy to care for our Mother.

We are inherently connected to Earth Mother and the day we realize this as a society, is the day we begin to change our behaviors.

We humans have ravaged our own Mother — destroyed our environment in so many ways — in our never-ending search for power and security.

This search is founded in our primal need for survival and it subsequent fear. It's an old fear and a fallacy at best. We've polluted our oceans, destroyed habitats for animals, and ruined the air quality of the world with our dream of power and security.

Our dream have turned into a nightmare, and now we are hurting ourselves, our chances for survival, and the countless species which inhabit our beautiful planet. This old dream shows us the depth of how unconscious we are as a species.

When we look at our world we can see how lost humanity is as a race.

It is also plain to see that we need to change our course if we are to survive and not only leave a wake of death and pollution in our tracks.

In shamanism we talk about dreaming our lives into existence. When we realize that we are the dreamer of our life, we also can take full responsibility for our situation and practice dreaming a new dream.

It's time for a new dream.

For Ourselves and Earth Mother.

What will it be?

The answer is up to You and me.

In remembrance of who and what we are, with immense Love and Gratitude to Pachamama and to You. Marcus

Page 94

Foot notes:

1. p. 5 - Masaru Emoto, Japanese Author and researcher. "The Hidden Messages In Water".

2. p. 7 - Bruce Lipton, PhD, American biologist and DNA researcher. **www.brucelipton.com**

3. p. 11 - Konrad Lorenz, Austrian zoologist.

4. p. 50 - DNA communicates with light
https://www.pnas.org/content/early/
2016/08/16/1602202113
Study to be found on **www.naturelovesme.com**

RESEARCH ARTICLE
Superresolution intrinsic fluorescence imaging of chromatin utilizing native, unmodified nucleic acids for contrast
Biqin Dong, Luay M. Almassalha, Yolanda Stypula-Cyrus, Ben E. Urban, John E. Chandler, The-Quyen Nguyen, Cheng Sun, Hao F. Zhang, and Vadim Backman
PNAS first published August 17, 2016;
https://doi.org/10.1073/pnas.1602202113

5. p. 50 - Photonic Communications and Information Encoding in Biological Systems
S.N. Mayburov
https://arxiv.org/abs/1205.4134

About the Author

Marcus Nobreus, born in Sweden, residing in Los Angeles. He also lived many many years in Mammoth Lakes, in the mountains of the Eastern Sierras. He had a spiritual awakening in 2010 after an encounter with the absolute stillness inside. Since then he has worked with healing many people, taught meditations, written movies, assisted people on their spiritual journey and engulfed himself on a Shamanic journey. He is taught by Sandra "Ombute" Beddor, a Shamanic practitioner in California. Learn more at www.healingwithmarcus.com and keep on the lookout for the next coming title: A Year of Peace. Daily Meditations and Insights.